The Arkansas River
The Colorado River
The Columbia River
The Mississippi River
The Missouri River

The Ohio River
The Red River
The Rio Grande River
The Snake River
The Yukon River

AMERICA'S TOP

10

RIVERS

By
Jenny Tesar

Published by Blackbirch Press, Inc.
260 Amity Road
Woodbridge, CT 06525

©1998 Blackbirch Press, Inc.
First Edition

Printed in the USA

10 9 8 7 6 5 4 3 2 1

Library of Congress Cataloging-in-Publication Data

Tesar, Jenny E.
  America's top 10 rivers / by Jenny Tesar.
      p. cm.—(America's top 10)
  Includes bibliographical references and index.
  Summary: Explores ten unique rivers in the United States, including the Mississippi,
Yukon and Rio Grande.
  ISBN 1-56711-189-0 (lib. bdg. : alk. paper)
  1. Rivers—United States—Juvenile literature. [1. Rivers] I. Title. II. Series.
GB1215.T475 1998
551.48'3'0973—dc21   96–38042
                                                                                                                CIP
                                                                                                                AC

B L A C K B I R C H   P R E S S ,   I N C.
W O O D B R I D G E ,   C O N N E C T I C U T

AMERICA'S TOP
10
RIVERS

Arkansas River

The
Arkansas River

The Arkansas River is one of the major tributaries (offshoots) of the Mississippi. It forms in the Rocky Mountains of central Colorado and flows eastward into Kansas. From Wichita, Kansas, the river turns southeast, flowing through Oklahoma and across central Arkansas. North of Arkansas City, the waters empty into the Mississippi.

The Arkansas descends more than 2 miles in elevation from source to mouth. Along the way, dams are used to provide flood control, crop irrigation, and electric power.

In Colorado, the river flows rapidly through the stunning Royal Gorge Canyon. The canyon's steep granite walls are spanned by the highest suspension bridge in America, the Royal Gorge Bridge. The Arkansas's rushing waters slow down at the Pueblo Reservoir. Visitors to this calm lake are surrounded by limestone cliffs and snow-capped mountain views.

In Kansas, the river widens and moves more slowly. It flows through prairies where millions of bison, or buffalo, once roamed. Today, these prairies are one of America's major wheat-producing regions. Corn and alfalfa also are raised here, thanks to irrigation water from the Arkansas. Cattle ranches are common on the prairies, too. Another important industry—petroleum—centers around the oil and natural gas fields found in the Arkansas River valley in Kansas and Oklahoma. The lower part of the river was widened in the early 1970s to allow barges and other boats to travel upstream as far as Tulsa, Oklahoma—the largest city on the river.

Name: From a Quapaw Indian word meaning "downstream people"

Location: Central United States

Length and rank: 1,459 miles; 4th longest

Source: Sawatch Range of the Rocky Mountains, Colorado

Flows into: Mississippi River

Major tributaries: Cimarron, Verdigris, and Canadian Rivers

Drainage area: 161,000 square miles

Major cities: Pueblo, CO; Wichita, KS; Tulsa, OK; Fort Smith and Little Rock, AR

Fun fact: In the late 1800s, legendary gunslingers Bat Masterson and Wyatt Earp were peace officers of Dodge City, Kansas, on the Arkansas River.

Opposite page:
The Arkansas provides water for many crops in the Arkansas River valley.

AMERICA'S TOP

10

RIVERS

Colorado River

NV
UT
WY
NE
CA
CO
AZ
NM
TX
MEXICO

The
Colorado River

★ ★ ★ ★ ★ ★ ★ ★ ★ ★ ★ ★ ★ ★

The Colorado River is the longest river west of the Rocky Mountains. It begins as a narrow stream in the Rocky Mountains in north-central Colorado. The river then flows southwest into Utah and northern Arizona and turns south, forming Arizona's borders with Nevada and California. Shortly after it passes Yuma, Arizona, the Colorado River enters Mexico. It empties into the Gulf of California, which is part of the Pacific Ocean.

The Colorado River has created some of the world's most spectacular scenery through the process of erosion (wearing away). For the past 6 million years, its flowing water has cut deep canyons into the rock. One of these is the Grand Canyon, which is 277 miles long, as much as 18 miles wide, and more than 1 mile deep.

The Colorado flows over more than 1,400 miles. Along the way, more than 50 rivers empty into it. Most of this water never reaches the Colorado's mouth because the water is used by cities and farmlands along the banks. Many dams have been built on the Colorado. The largest is Hoover Dam, on the border of Nevada and Arizona. Generators there provide electricity to Arizona, Nevada, and southern California.

In southern California, much of the Colorado's water is directed into the All-American Canal. About 80 miles long and 200 feet wide, this is the largest irrigation canal in the United States. It supplies water to the Imperial Valley, which was once desert. Today, citrus fruits, melons, cotton, and many other crops are grown there.

Name: From Spanish words meaning "reddish color"

Location: Southwestern United States and northern Mexico

Length and rank: 1,450 miles; 5th longest

Source: Rocky Mountain National Park, Colorado

Flows into: Gulf of California

Major U.S. tributaries: Gunnison, Dolores, Green, San Juan, Little Colorado, and Gila Rivers

Drainage area: 244,000 square miles

Major cities: Grand Junction, CO; Yuma, AZ

Fun fact: In 1996, an artificial flood was created where the Colorado River flows through the Grand Canyon to improve living conditions for rare fish, such as humpback chubs.

Opposite page:
The Colorado River has carved dramatic canyons in America's Southwest.

AMERICA'S TOP

10

RIVERS

CANADA

WA

MI

Columbia River

OR

ID

CO

CA

NV

UT

The
Columbia River

The Columbia River starts at Columbia Lake, among the snow-capped Rocky Mountains in western Canada. It enters the United States in northeastern Washington and flows generally in a southerly direction to the Oregon border. It then flows west to the Pacific, forming the border between Washington and Oregon.

At one time, roaring rapids were common along the Columbia. The construction of numerous dams, however, has slowed the river. These dams provide electricity for homes and industries, water for irrigation, and protection against flooding. They also allow boats to travel more than 400 miles upriver from the mouth.

The largest of the dams is Grand Coulee, in northwestern Washington. One of the largest concrete structures in the world, it is 550 feet high and 5,223 feet long. Behind it, the Columbia widens to form Franklin D. Roosevelt Lake, which is 150 miles long.

The Bonneville Dam is on the Washington-Oregon Border. Visitors there can view fish ladders through underwater windows. A fish ladder consists of a series of pools alongside the dam. Each is slightly higher than the one below. They are designed to allow salmon to bypass the dam as they swim up the Columbia to their breeding grounds.

Before the dams were built and industries polluted the water, huge numbers of salmon swam in the Columbia. Now, to increase the population, young salmon are raised in fish hatcheries, and then released into the river.

Name: Named for his ship, "Columbia Rediviva," by the American trader Robert Gray, who explored the river's mouth in 1792

Location: Southwestern Canada and northwestern United States

Length and rank: 1,240 miles; 8th longest

Source: Columbia Lake, British Columbia, Canada

Flows into: Pacific Ocean

Major U.S. tributaries: Kootenay, Snake, and Willamette Rivers

Drainage area: 258,000 square miles

Major cities: Portland, OR; Vancouver, WA

Fun fact: In 1966, a salmon hatchery next to Bonneville Dam hatched 15 million salmon. About 1 percent of the fish survived to adulthood.

Opposite page:
The Columbia River flows through the beautiful landscape of the Pacific Northwest.

AMERICA'S TOP

10

RIVERS

MT | ND | | CANADA
WY | SD | MN | WI
CO | NE | IA | MI | NY
| KS | MO | IL | IN | OH | WV | PA
NM | | OK | AR | KY | VA
Mississippi River | TN | NC
TX | | MS | AL | GA | SC
MEXICO | LA | FL

The
Mississippi River

★ ★ ★ ★ ★ ★ ★ ★ ★ ★ ★ ★ ★ ★ ★ ★ ★

The "Mighty Mississippi" is America's main river drainage system. Rivers in 31 states are connected to it, either directly or indirectly. All together, the Mississippi River system drains water from about 40 percent of the United States as well as parts of central Canada.

The Mississippi begins at Lake Itasca, Minnesota. There it is only about 12 feet wide and 1.5 feet deep. As the river flows south and is joined by tributaries, it grows wider and deeper—up to 5,000 feet wide and 12 feet deep. The lower part of the river meanders, or bends continuously. As a result, the length of the river between Cairo, Illinois, and New Orleans, Louisiana, is almost 3 times that of the valley.

The Mississippi carries huge amounts of sediment. The river bottom is constantly dredged (cleared) to remove this sediment and maintain a channel deep enough for navigation. As the river empties into the Gulf of Mexico, it deposits the sediment. Over thousands of years, this sediment has created fertile new land, called a delta.

In the spring, when snow melts and rainfall is heavy, the quantity of water carried by the Mississippi increases dramatically. To protect the surrounding towns against flooding, many dams and levees have been built along the river. This protection is not always enough, however. In the Great Flood of 1993, the river rose so high that it burst through the dams and levees. The floodwaters caused enormous damage to local crops and property.

Name: From an Algonquian Indian word meaning "father of waters"
Location: Central United States
Length and rank: 2,340 miles; longest
Source: Lake Itasca, Minnesota
Flows into: Gulf of Mexico
Major tributaries: Iowa, Des Moines, Illinois, Missouri, Ohio, St. Francis, Arkansas and Red Rivers
Drainage area: 1.2 million square miles
Major cities: Minneapolis—Saint Paul, MN; Saint Louis, MO; Cairo, IL; Memphis, TN; Natchez, MS; Baton Rouge and New Orleans, LA
Fun fact: Tourists enjoy riding on replicas of the steamboats that carried passengers along the river in the late 19th century.

Opposite page:
Barges travel up and down the wide Mississippi.

AMERICA'S TOP

10

RIVERS

CANADA

MI

ND

Missouri River

MN

ID

WY

SD

WI

NE

IA

UT

CO

IL

AZ

NM

KS

MO

The
Missouri River

The "Mighty Mo" is the largest tributary of the Mississippi River. It originates at Three Forks, Montana, where the Jefferson, Gallatin, and Madison Rivers join together. The Missouri flows 2,714 miles from the Rocky Mountains to the Mississippi. On its journey, it flows through, or runs along the borders of, 7 states: Montana, North Dakota, South Dakota, Nebraska, Iowa, Kansas, and Missouri.

Near its source, the Missouri flows through mountainous terrain covered with evergreen forests where bear, elk, and moose live. Outside Helena, Montana, it flows through the deep, scenic gorge, Gates of the Mountains. Soon after, the river tumbles over a series of waterfalls, dropping 400 feet in 12 miles. Then the river broadens, its volume increased by water from many tributaries.

For most of its length, the Missouri flows through the Great Plains. Cattle and grain crops are raised in the fertile soil near the river. Trees such as poplar and hickory are common.

Dams built on the river have created several huge lakes, including Fort Peck Reservoir in Montana and Lake Sakakawea in North Dakota. These dams are used to control flooding, generate electricity, irrigate farmland, and provide recreation.

The Missouri has always been used for transportation. Native Americans traveled the river in canoes to trade with one another. Today, river traffic includes many tugboats pushing barges that carry grain, oil, and other products.

Name: From an Illinois Native American word meaning "dwellers of the big muddy"
Location: Central United States
Length and rank: 2,315 miles; 2nd longest
Source: Jefferson, Madison, and Gallatin Rivers
Flows into: Mississippi River
Major tributaries: Little Missouri, Cheyenne, James, Platte, and Kansas Rivers
Drainage area: 592,000 square miles
Major cities: Great Falls, MT; Bismarck, ND; Pierre, SD; Sioux City, IA; Omaha, NE; Kansas City, KS; Jefferson City, MO; and Saint Louis, MO
Fun fact: The Missouri carries so much sediment that people have nicknamed it Big Muddy.

Opposite page:
South Dakota's rolling hills are part of the scenery along the Missouri River.

AMERICA'S TOP

10

RIVERS

WI | MI | CANADA | NY
IL | IN | OH | PA
| | Ohio River | WV | VA
| KY | |
TN | NC

The
Ohio River

★ ★ ★ ★ ★ ★ ★ ★ ★ ★ ★ ★ ★ ★ ★

The Ohio River starts in the middle of Pittsburgh, Pennsylvania, where it is surrounded by skyscrapers. There, the Allegheny and Monongahela Rivers come together at Point State Park. A giant fountain in the park symbolizes the joining of the two rivers to form the Ohio.

The Ohio River generally flows southwest, running along the borders of West Virginia, Ohio, Kentucky, Indiana, and Illinois. It joins the Mississippi River at Cairo, Illinois. The Ohio is the largest eastern tributary of the Mississippi.

The river is lined by steep bluffs for most of its length. In some places, beautiful forests of oak, hickory, and maple grow along the banks. White-tailed deer, squirrels, and pheasants populate these forests.

The river's upper valley is home to many industries. Soap, ceramics, and home appliances are among the many products manufactured there. The lower valley is dotted with farms where corn, soybeans, and tobacco are grown.

In Louisville, Kentucky, are the attractive rapids known as the Falls of the Ohio. Here, the river's elevation drops almost 24 feet in 2.5 miles. A canal was built around the rapids in 1830, allowing boats to move up and down the river.

The entire Ohio is navigable, thanks to dams and locks. Most of the river traffic consists of barges carrying coal that is mined nearby. All the states along the Ohio have coal mines. The coal is taken to power plants, where it is burned to produce electricity.

Name: From the Iroquois words meaning "beautiful river"
Location: East-central United States
Length and rank: 981 miles; 10th longest
Source: Allegheny and Monongahela Rivers in Pittsburgh, Pennsylvania
Flows into: Mississippi River
Major tributaries: Beaver, Scioto, Kentucky, Green, Wabash, and Tennessee Rivers
Drainage area: 203,000 square miles
Major cities: Pittsburgh, PA; Cincinnati, OH; Louisville, KY; Evansville, IN; and Paducah, KY
Fun fact: The city of Louisville, Kentucky, on the banks of the Ohio, is the original home of the famous Louisville Slugger baseball bats.

Opposite page:
The bright lights of Cincinnati's waterfront glitter on the Ohio River.

AMERICA'S TOP

10

RIVERS

OK

AR

Red River

TX

MS

LA

The
Red River

★ ★ ★ ★ ★ ★ ★ ★ ★ ★ ★ ★ ★ ★ ★ ★

The Red River forms much of the border between Oklahoma and Texas as well as part of the border between Texas and Arkansas. It flows southeast through Louisiana. About 11 miles before it joins the Mississippi, it divides into two rivers, called the Old River and the Atchafalaya River. The Old River flows into the Mississippi. The Atchafalaya flows south, emptying into the Gulf of Mexico. The Red can be navigated from the Gulf as far inland as Fulton, Arkansas.

The Red River system begins with Tierra Blanca Creek in eastern New Mexico. Hundreds of miles to the east, the creek's waters mingle with those of other creeks and rivers to form Prairie Dog Town Fork. In Oklahoma, this river merges with the North Fork Red River and becomes the Red River. The Red River flows through rolling plains of red clay, which gives the water its color—and the river its name.

Dams on the river protect the nearby land against flooding and provide water for irrigation. Along the Texas-Oklahoma border, much of the Red River valley is used for raising cattle and for growing wheat.

Lake Texoma, formed by Denison Dam, is about 70 miles north of Dallas. Other popular lakes are found in Louisiana, where the Red River's changing course has created cutoff lakes in the soft soil. These lakes often start out as U-shaped loops called "oxbows." When separated from the river—perhaps because the river has found another path—oxbows become cutoff lakes.

Name: From the water's reddish color

Location: South-central United States

Length and rank: 1,018 miles; 6th longest

Source: North Fork Red River and Prairie Dog Town Fork

Flows into: Mississippi and Atchafalaya Rivers

Major tributaries: Pease, Wichita, Tashita, Kiamichi, and Sulphur Rivers

Drainage area: 93,200 square miles

Major cities: Shreveport, LA; Alexandria, LA

Fun fact: The Red River valley in Louisiana is a major cotton-growing region.

Opposite page:
The red clay soil over which the river flows colors the water.

AMERICA'S TOP

10

RIVERS

UT CO KS MO

AZ NM OK AR

TX MS

LA

Rio Grande

MEXICO

The Rio Grande River

The Rio Grande begins at an elevation of more than 12,000 feet in the mountains of southwestern Colorado. It tumbles downward as it travels eastward to Alamosa, Colorado. There, it turns south and flows through New Mexico to Texas, where it forms the border between Texas and Mexico. It then empties into the Gulf of Mexico.

The river has cut deep canyons in the flatlands of New Mexico. Rio Grande Gorge is 50 miles long and 800 feet deep. The walls of the gorge rise almost vertically from the river's edge. Further south is Bosque del Apache National Wildlife Refuge, home to many bobcats, deer, coyotes, and other wild animals. Many migrating birds spend the winter there—or use the refuge as a stopping place before continuing on their journey farther south.

From El Paso, in the westernmost part of Texas, to the Gulf of Mexico, the Rio Grande is an international waterway. Bridges connect cities in Texas with sister communities in Mexico. Americans and Mexicans alike enjoy the Amistad Reservoir, west of Del Rio, Texas. Overlooking the dam that forms this lake is a huge stone statue of Tlaloc, the Aztec rain god.

During most of the year, the Rio Grande carries little water. It has been dammed in many places to provide electricity, flood control, and water for irrigation. Farming is important in much of the Rio Grande valley. In southern New Mexico, crops such as pecans, cotton, onions, and lettuce are grown.

Name: Spanish for "great river"

Location: Southwestern United States and northern Mexico

Length and rank: 1,885 miles; 3rd longest

Source: Rocky Mountains in western Colorado

Flows into: Gulf of Mexico

Major U.S. tributaries: Chama, Puerco, Pecos, and Devils Rivers

Drainage area: 172,000 square miles

Major U.S. cities: Albuquerque, NM; El Paso, Laredo, and Brownsville, TX

Fun fact: In Mexico, this river is called Rio Bravo, meaning "brave river."

Opposite page:
The Rio Grande flows through the arid Texas desert.

WA

MT

OR

ID

Snake River

NV

UT

WY

The
Snake River

★ ★ ★ ★ ★ ★ ★ ★ ★ ★ ★ ★ ★ ★ ★ ★

The Snake River originates in Yellowstone National Park. From there, it twists and turns through Wyoming, Idaho, Oregon, and Washington. Near Pasco, Washington, it empties into the Columbia River. The Snake River is the largest tributary of the Columbia.

Soon after the Snake leaves Yellowstone, it flows through Grand Teton National Park. There, it widens and forms Jackson Lake. Evergreen forests and colorful wildflower meadows line the banks of the lake.

In southeastern Idaho, the Snake River has cut a deep valley in the earth, forming steep canyons and many rapids and waterfalls. Among the most beautiful of these is Shoshone Falls, where the river plunges 212 feet over a horseshoe-shaped rim that is 900 feet wide.

As the Snake River crosses southern Idaho, it provides water for the famous Idaho potatoes, as well as for beans, wheat, and other crops. At the western side of the state, the Snake suddenly turns northward, forming much of the border between Idaho and Oregon. There, it flows through the 100-mile-long Hells Canyon—the deepest river gorge in the nation. With a depth of 7,900 feet, it is some 1,500 feet deeper than the Grand Canyon!

At Lewiston, Idaho, the Snake turns towards the west, flowing through southeastern Washington, where it is regulated by dams. To the river's north is a large wheat-growing area. The Snake is also a popular river for fishing. It is filled with many fish varieties, especially salmon.

Name: Named by European settlers who misinterpreted Shoshone sign language for "fish" to mean "snake."
Location: Northwestern United States
Length and rank: 1,040 miles; 9th longest
Source: Yellowstone National Park, Wyoming
Flows into: Columbia River
Major tributaries: Wind, Bruneau, Salmon, Powder, Clearwater, and Palouse Rivers
Drainage area: 108,000 square miles
Major cities: Idaho Falls and Lewiston, ID
Fun fact: The Snake River was used by pioneers traveling the Oregon Trail.

Opposite page:
The Snake River travels through many canyons on its journey from Wyoming to Washington.

AMERICA'S TOP

10

RIVERS

AK

CANADA

Yukon River

The Yukon River

The Yukon begins in mountains in Yukon Territory and British Columbia. It flows northwest to Fort Yukon, Alaska. Then it flows in a southwesterly direction across a broad, tree-covered plain towards the Bering Sea. The river carries enormous amounts of sediment that it deposits in the sea. As a result, the river has created one of the world's largest deltas. About 50 small Inuit villages are located on the delta.

Winters in the Yukon are long and cold, with short periods of daylight. Much of this region freezes from October to June. In summer, when the river floods, millions of birds nest in the Yukon Delta National Wildlife Refuge.

The most famous area along the Yukon River is in Canada. In 1896, gold was discovered in some of the creeks that empty into the Klondike River, near where it joins with the Yukon. Thousands of people rushed to the area in the hope of becoming rich. At the fork where the two rivers meet, the town of Dawson was born. In just 2 years, its population grew to 16,000 people. Within a few years, however, gold production dropped and most people left the area.

Relatively few people live along the Yukon today, but the land surrounding the river is rich in wildlife. Grizzly bears, wolverines, lynx, marten, mink, and large herds of reindeer live there. The river is full of salmon and other fish.

At one time, the river was the main means of transportation in the Alaskan interior and the Yukon Territory. But today, the river is used mostly for local travel.

Name: From Inuit Eskimo words meaning "great river"
Location: Canada and Alaska
Length and rank (in U.S.): 1,265 miles; 7th longest
Source: Lakes in Yukon Territory and British Columbia, Canada
Flows into: Bering Sea
Major U.S. tributaries: Porcupine, Tanana, Koyukuk, and Innoko Rivers
Drainage area: 328,000 square miles
Major U.S. cities: none
Fun fact: A rare bird called the "bristle-thighed curlew" spends the summer on the Yukon Delta. Then it flies to the South Pacific, over 2,000 miles away, for the winter.

Opposite page:
The Yukon River floods every summer and covers the surrounding plain.

America's Top 10 Rivers are the longest in the country. Below is a list of the major rivers in the United States.

America's Major Rivers

State: Rivers

Alabama: Alabama, Chattahoochee, Mobile, Tennessee, Tombigbee

Alaska: Cooper, Koyukuk, Kuskokwin, Porcupine, Susitna, Tanana, Yukon

Arizona: Colorado, Gila, Little Colorado, Santa Cruz

Arkansas: Arkansas, Black, Buffalo, Mississippi, Red

California: American, Colorado, Eel, Klamath, Sacramento, San Joaquin, Trinity

Colorado: Arkansas, Colorado, North Platte, Rio Grande, South Platte

Connecticut: Connecticut, Housatonic, Naugatuck, Thames

Delaware: Christina, Delaware, Indian, Mispillion, Nanticoke

Florida: Apalachicola, Caloosahatchee, Kissimmee, St. Johns, St. Marys, Suwannee

Georgia: Altamaha, Chattahoochee, Flint, Ogeechee, Satilla, Savannah

Hawaii: None

Idaho: Bear, Boise, Clearwater, Couer d'Alene, Salmon, Snake

Illinois: Green, Illinois, Mississippi, Ohio, Wabash

Indiana: Eel, Mississinewa, Ohio, Patoka, Tippecanoe, Wabash

Iowa: Cedar, Des Moines, Iowa, Little Sioux, Mississippi, Missouri, Skunk, Wapsipinicon

Kansas: Arkansas, Kansas, Missouri, Neosho, Saline, Smoky Hill, Solomon, Verdigris

Kentucky: Green, Kentucky, Licking, Mississippi, Ohio, Tennessee

Louisiana: Calcasieu, Mississippi, Ouachita, Pearl, Red, Sabine

Maine: Androscoggin, Kennebec, Penobscot, St. Croix, St. John

Maryland: Monacacy, Pocomoke, Potomac, Youghiogheny

Massachusetts: Charles, Concord, Connecticut, Deerfield, Housatonic, Merrimack, Tauton

Michigan: Detroit, Grand, Menominee, Muskegon, St. Clair, St. Marys

Minnesota: Minnesota, Mississippi, Red River of the North, St. Croix, St. Louis

Mississippi: Big Black, Chickasawhay, Mississippi, Pearl, Tombigbee, Yazoo

Missouri: Current, Gasconade, Meramec, Mississippi, Missouri, Osage, Salt, St. Francis

Montana: Jefferson, Madison, Marias, Missouri, Musselshell, Powder, Tongue, Yellowstone

Nebraska: Big Blue, Elkhorn, Little Blue, Loup, Niobrara, Platte, Republican

Nevada: Carson, Colorado, Humboldt, Reese, Truckee

New Hampshire: Androscoggin, Connecticut, Merrimack, Piscataqua, Saco, Salmon Falls

New Jersey: Hackensack, Maurice, Passaic, Raritan

New Mexico: Canadian, Gila, Pecos, Rio Grande, San Juan

New York: Delaware, Genesee, Hudson, Mohawk, Niagara, St. Lawrence, Susquehanna

North Carolina: Cape Fear, Catawba, Neuse, Roanoke, Tar-Pamlico, Yadkin-Pee Dee

North Dakota: Cedar, James, Little Missouri, Missouri, Sheyenne, Souris

Ohio: Cuyahoga, Great Miami, Little Miami, Muskingum, Ohio, Sandusky, Scioto

Oklahoma: Arkansas, Canadian, Cimarron, Red, Verdigris

Oregon: Columbia, John Day, Rogue, Snake, Umpqua, Willamette

Pennsylvania: Allegheny, Delaware, Lehigh, Monongahela, Schuylkill, Susquehanna

Rhode Island: Blackstone, Pawtucket

South Carolina: Broad, Edisto, Lynches, Pee Dee, Santee, Savannah

South Dakota: Bad, Big Sioux, Cheyenne, James, Missouri, Moreau, Vermillion, White

Tennessee: Cumberland, Duck, Hatchie, Mississippi, Tennessee

Texas: Brazos, Canadian, Colorado, Pecos, Red, Rio Grande, Sabine, Trinity

Utah: Bear, Colorado, Green, Jordan, Provo, San Juan, Weber

Vermont: Lamoille, Missisquoi, West, White, Winooski

Virginia: Clinch, Dan, James, New, Potomac, Rappahannock, Roanoke, Shenandoah, York

Washington: Columbia, Skagit, Snake, Spokane, Yakima

West Virginia: Big Sandy, Guyandotte, Greenbrier, Kanawha, Monongahela, Ohio, Potomac

Wisconsin: Black, Chippewa, Fox, Mississippi, Rock, St. Croix, Wisconsin, Wolf

Wyoming: Belle Fourche, Bighorn, Cheyenne, Green, North Platte, Powder, Snake, Yellowstone

Glossary

bluff A steep river bank.

canyon A narrow passage with steep rocky sides, formed by a river.

dam A barrier built across a river. Dams are built to control the flow of water or to raise the water level.

delta A deposit of soil and other sediment at the mouth of a river.

drainage area The land that contributes water to a river and all its tributaries.

dredge To deepen or widen a river, using a machine called a dredge.

elevation Height above sea level.

erode To wear away slowly by the action of water, wind, or glacial ice.

levee A mound built along a river bank to prevent the river from overflowing.

lock A section of a river closed off with gates. Boats can be raised or lowered by raising or lowering the water level in the lock.

meander To follow a turning or winding course.

mouth The place where a river empties into a larger body of water.

navigable Deep enough and wide enough for boat travel.

rapids The place where a riverbed descends steeply, causing the water to move fast.

reservoir An artificial lake created by a dam.

river system All the streams and rivers that empty their water—directly or indirectly—into a major river.

sediment Particles of soil and other materials carried by flowing water and eventually deposited.

source The place where a river begins.

tributary A river that flows into a larger one.

Further Reading

Ayer, Eleanor. *Our Great Rivers and Waterways.* Brookfield, CT: Millbrook Press, 1994.

Bailey, Donna. *Rivers.* Austin, TX: Raintree Steck-Vaughn, 1990.

Clifford, Nick. *Incredible Earth.* New York: Dorling Kindersley, 1996.

Cooper, Jason. *The Mississippi Delta.* Vero Beach, FL: Rourke, 1995.

Louri, Peter. *In the Path of Lewis & Clark: Traveling the Missouri.* Parsippany, NJ: Silver Burdett, 1996.

Mariner, Tom. *Rivers.* Tarrytown, NY: Marshall Cavendish, 1990.

Morgan, Nina. *The Mississippi.* Austin, TX: Raintree Steck-Vaughn, 1993.

Palmer, Tim. *The Wind and Scenic Rivers of America.* Fort Myers Beach, FL: Island Press, 1993.

Where to Get On-Line Information

The Colorado River http://river.ihs.gov

The Mississippi River http://www.greatriver.com

The Missouri River http://www.esu3.k12.ne.us/districts/ralston/hs/river/thriverboats.html

The Yukon River http://cesdis.gsfc.nasa.gov/people/becker/yukon.html

Index

Photo Credits

Cover and page 2: ©Carl M. Purcell '95/Photo Researchers, Inc.; cover and page 4: ©George Ranall/Photo Researchers, Inc.; cover and page 6: ©Steve Terrill/Oregon Tourism; cover and page 8: Louisiana Office of Tourism; cover and page 10: Photo by South Dakota Tourism; cover and page 12; ©92 Elder Photo/Call 1-800-BUCKEYE for Ohio Travel Information; cover and page 14: Courtesy of Red River Waterway Commission; cover and page 16: ©Gary Retherford/Photo Researchers, Inc.; cover and page 18: PhotoDisc, Inc.; cover and page 20: ©Steve Krasema/Photo Researchers, Inc.